what about...
world
wonders?

what about...
world
wonders?

Brian Williams

Miles
Kelly
PUBLISHING

First published in 2005 by Miles Kelly Publishing Ltd
Harding's Barn, Bardfield End Green, Thaxted, Essex, CM6 3PX

This edition printed in 2011 by Miles Kelly Publishing Ltd

Copyright © 2005 Miles Kelly Publishing Ltd

4 6 8 10 9 7 5

British Library Cataloguing-in-Publication Data
A catalogue record for this book is available from the British Library

ISBN 978-1-84236-796-4

Printed in China

Editorial Director Belinda Gallagher
Art Director Jo Brewer
Assistant Editors Lucy Dowling, Rosalind McGuire
Design Concept John Christopher
Volume Designers Jo Brewer, Tony Collins
Picture Researchers Laura Faulder, Liberty Newton
Indexer Jane Parker
Production Manager Elizabeth Collins
Reprographics Anthony Cambray, Liberty Newton, Ian Paulyn

www.mileskelly.net
info@mileskelly.net

www.factsforprojects.com

CONTENTS

Wonders of the Ancient World   8–9

What was the Mausoleum?
Which god became a Wonder?
Which Wonder had a fire on top?
Who was honoured in the Temple at Ephesus?
Which is the most mysterious Wonder?
Which Wonder was sold off for scrap?

Puzzling Pyramids   10–11

Why were the Great Pyramids built?
Who thought pyramids were a waste of money?
How many pyramids are there?
How were pyramids built?
Where else were pyramids built?
What is a step pyramid?

Marvels of Greece and Rome   12–13

Why did the Greeks build temples?
Which Roman town disappeared under hot ash?
Where is the Acropolis?
Which Roman column tells stories?
Why did the Romans build aqueducts?
How did the Colosseum get its name?
Which Roman wonder had a hole in it?

Mysterious Monuments   14–15

Why did ancient peoples build circles of stone?
Where is the Great Serpent Mound?
Which Pacific island has the strangest statues?
Why does Stonehenge fascinate people?
Where are there strange pictures in a desert?

Forts and Castles   16–17

What was Maiden Castle?
Who built Britain's strongest castles?
What is the Krak des Chevaliers?
Where is the Red Fort?
Which castle sits on a volcano?
Where is Great Zimbabwe?

Palaces and Power   18–19

Walls and Towers   20–21

Built for Eternity   22–23

Technological Triumphs   24–25

Engineering Marvels   26–27

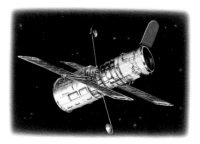

Memorials and Mysteries

What was unearthed at Sutton Hoo?
Whose journey is remembered by a giant arch?
Who was buried with an army of clay soldiers?
Whose tomb revealed a lost treasure?
Which leaders stare out from a mountain?
Where did the last Incas live in secret?

Awesome Landscapes

Where are the world's mightiest mountains?
Which is the strangest lake?
Where is the thickest ice?
Where is Monument Valley?
Where are there too many trees to count?
Which is the world's biggest desert?

Stupendous Sights

What makes the Grand Canyon so grand?
Which waterfall is higher than a skyscraper?
Which is America's most destructive volcano?
Which is Australia's biggest pebble?
Which is the longest coral reef?

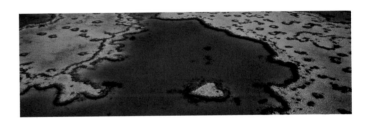

Nature's Record Breakers

Which is the fastest land animal?
Where is the most massive tree?
Why are termites so astounding?
Which animal gives birth to the biggest baby?
Which is the biggest of all the big cats?
How many kinds of elephant are there?

Seven stupendous structures, built between 3000 and 200 BC, became known as the Seven Wonders of the Ancient World. Tourists of old had to travel what were then vast and difficult distances – across Europe, North Africa and eastern Asia. This was the 'civilized world', as known to the Greeks and Romans, who first listed the 'Seven Wonders'.

⬆ *The word 'mausoleum' came to mean a large tomb.*

What was the Mausoleum?

This was a marble tomb built about 353 BC at Halicarnassus, in what is now southwestern Turkey. It was commissioned for Mausolus, who was ruler of a province in the Persian Empire. The beautiful tomb was created by architects and sculptors from Greece. High on the roof, over 40 m from the ground, a statue was built of King Mausolus driving in his chariot.

Which god became a Wonder?

Zeus, king of the gods who the ancient Greeks believed lived on Mount Olympus. A mighty statue of Zeus at Olympia was 12 m high (six times human-size) and was made of ivory and gold. People visited the god's temple to marvel at the statue of Zeus, made about 435 BC by Phidias, the greatest sculptor of ancient Greece.

⬆ *Zeus was seated on a golden throne, wearing a robe and ornaments of gold.*

⬆ *The Pharos at Alexandria was so famous that the word pharos came to mean 'lighthouse'.*

Which Wonder had a fire on top?

The Pharos or Lighthouse at Alexandria (Egypt). It was a huge tower, built on an island as a lighthouse to guide ships in and out of the harbour. The lighthouse was 122 m high, and workers kept a fire burning at the top to provide the light. The first lighthouse in history, it stood for about 1,500 years.

Wonders of their **time**

Famous monuments

Had the compilers of the ancient wonders known about the Great Wall of China (see page 20 for more information), they would have added an eighth wonder. But China was too far away.

The shortest-lived Ancient Wonder was the Colossus of Rhodes. It stood for less than 20 years before being toppled by an earthquake.

The Temple of Artemis burned down in 356 BC. A second temple built on the same site was also destroyed by fire, in AD 262. Sculptures from this second temple's ruins were later taken to the British Museum in London.

Not much is left of the Mausoleum. It fell in an earthquake, but a few chunks and some sculptures survive.

The Great Sphinx is so old that sand blowing in the wind has rubbed away detail of the lion's body and parts of Khafre's face.

To water the Hangng Gardens, slaves worked in shifts, lifting water from the Euphrates River.

➡ *China's Great Wall was not known to Europeans until after the AD 1200s, when Marco Polo visited China.*

→ *Water was pumped from the Euphrates River to water the flowers and trees on the Hanging Garden's terraces.*

Which Wonder was sold off for scrap?

A huge bronze statue, which stood at the harbour of Rhodes, an island in the Aegean Sea. A figure of the Sun god Helios, standing about 27 m tall, it was called the Colossus of Rhodes. The builders used stone blocks and iron bars to hold up the hollow figure. The iron was sold off as scrap metal in the AD 600s, 800 years after the Colossus was toppled by an earthquake.

↓ *The people of Rhodes made the Colossus to celebrate their victory against invaders in the 200s BC.*

Who was honoured in the Temple at Ephesus?

Artemis, a Greek goddess. In the city of Ephesus on the west coast of what is now Turkey stood a magnificent marble temple. The temple honoured Artemis, who in Greek mythology was the daughter of Zeus, king of the gods. She was the goddess of childbirth and also of wild animals and hunting.

← *The Temple of Artemis at Ephesus was finished in about 550 BC and rebuilt after a fire in 356 BC. It had 106 columns, which were each about 12 m high.*

Which is the most mysterious Wonder?

The Hanging Gardens of Babylon. The Gardens were probably near Baghdad in Iraq. Writing 400 years after the Gardens were built, a priest described them as being like a ziggurat (a pyramid) with terraces covered in trees and plants. One story says that King Nebuchadnezzar II ordered the Hanging Gardens to please one of his wives, who missed the greenery of her mountain home.

Seven **Wonders**

...and what happened to them

Temple of Artemis at Ephesus (Turkey) 500 BC. Burned down 356 BC.

Statue of Zeus at Olympia (Greece) 435 BC. Fate unknown.

The Lighthouse at Alexandria (Egypt) 283–246 BC. Collapsed AD 1300s.

The Colossus of Rhodes (Aegean Sea) about 210 BC. Fell down in an earthquake in 224 BC.

Hanging Gardens of Babylon (Iraq) late 500s BC. Fate unknown.

Mausoleum at Halicarnassus (Turkey) 353 BC. Fragments remain.

The Pyramids at Giza (Egypt) 2500–2600 BC. Still standing.

Of the Seven Wonders of the Ancient World, only the pyramids of Egypt remain in anything like their original splendour. The pyramids are the oldest of the Seven Wonders of the Ancient World, and the biggest.

⬆ *The royal burial chamber was reached by a passage deep inside the Great Pyramid.*

⬇ *The Great Pyramids stand at Giza beside the Nile River in Egypt.*

How many pyramids are there?

The ruins of 35 large pyramids can be seen today near the Nile River in Egypt. The most famous are three enormous pyramids that stand at Giza, near the capital city of Cairo. These pyramids were built for three very powerful kings of Egypt. Their names were Khufu, Khafre and Menkaure.

⬇ *The Great Pyramids stand at Giza beside the Nile River in Egypt.*

Why were the Great Pyramids built?

The pyramids were built as tombs for kings of Egypt. The Egyptians believed that their rulers would continue to live on after they had died. The pyramid tombs contained burial chambers inside which the dead king was placed, along with objects that he might need in the next world. Inside the Great Pyramid of King Khufu were sealed chambers full of treasure.

Who thought pyramids were a waste of money?

The ancient Romans. They were impressed by the size of the Egyptian pyramids, but they thought they were extravagant projects of Egyptian kings with too much wealth, too many slave-workers – and nothing better to do! The Romans spent their money on useful projects, such as the building of roads.

➡ *The three great pyramids were built about 4,500 years ago – about 2600 to 2500 BC.*

Pyramid facts

⬇ *The Great Sphinx has a human head, a lion's b wears a royal headdress.*

Mysterious pyramids
American pyramids were vast piles of earth, faced with stones, with temples on top. Egyptian pyramids were made entirely of stone, with tombs inside.

The largest Egyptian pyramid, Khufu's, was built with over two million stones.

Risking many different booby-traps, tomb-robbers managed to steal the treasures in almost all of the tombs.

Valley of the Kings
After 1700 BC, Egyptian kings were buried in rock tombs in the Valley of the Kings.

Tutankhamen's tomb is one of 62 royal tombs in or near the Valley of the Kings, on the west bank of the Nile River.

The Egyptians cut stones with copper tools – they had no iron. They had no machines either, relying on rollers, sledges, ropes and muscle power.

⬆ *Inside the Great Pyramid, a passage led to the burial chamber. Heavy stones sealed the passage to stop robbers breaking into the tomb.*

What is a step pyramid?

The first pyramid in ancient Egypt was built for King Zoser about 2650 BC and is called the Step Pyramid, because it rises in a series of giant steps. It stands at the site of the ancient city of Memphis, near Saqqarah. Later pyramids were faced with stones, which made each side smooth, though today the sides look rough and worn.

🔽 *The Step Pyramid looked like the ziggurat-temples built in Mesopotamia (present-day Iraq). Below ground, there is a warren of tunnels, galleries and rooms.*

How were pyramids built?

The Egyptians had no machinery or iron tools and so they cut huge blocks of stone with copper chisels and saws. Most of the stones came from quarries nearby, but others were brought by boat along the Nile River. Gangs of workers dragged the stones up long ramps of earth and brick as the pyramid slowly rose higher and higher. Finally, it was coated with white stones, to gleam brilliantly in the hot desert sun.

Where else were pyramids built?

There are pyramids in America too. People of Mexico and Central America built stepped pyramids with temples on top. The Pyramid of the Sun at Teotihuacan, Mexico, is bigger (in volume) than the Great Pyramid in Egypt. This huge pyramid is more than 1,500 years old. Ancient people in Peru in South America also built pyramids.

◀ *The Pyramid of the Sun was built by people who lived in Mexico, long before the Spanish conquerors came in the 1500s.*

The Great Sphinx
For thousands of years, people have come to stare at the statue of the Great Sphinx. This monument, half human and half animal, guards the pyramid of King Khafre. Some experts think the Great Sphinx is even older than the pyramids.

The Great Sphinx is 73 m long and about 20 m high.

The head and body were carved out of limestone rock. Part of the head is broken. Some historians believe Napoleon Bonaparte's soldiers shot at it for fun.

Over the years, the Great Sphinx has been buried up to its neck in sand many times.

Great pyramid **facts**

Base length (each side)	230 m
Area	5 hc
Number of stones	about 2.3 million
Average stone weight	over 2 tonnes
Biggest stone	290 tonnes
Labour force	100,000 workers toiling for 30 years

Huge stone statues of King Ramses II guarded the Great Temple at Abu Simbel near the Nile River. When the Aswan High Dam was built in the 1960s, engineers moved the 3000-year-old temple to higher ground so that it was not flooded by the rising waters.

The Greeks were famous for their skill at building, not only temples and palaces, but theatres and arenas too. They were also marvellous sculptors. The Romans copied Greek buildings, and made improvements – the dome, for instance. The Romans imitated the Greeks in making lifelike figures in bronze, marble, gold and ivory.

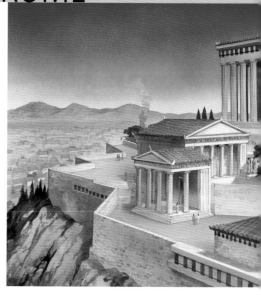

⬆ *The Parthenon stands on the Acropolis. Greeks thought the goddess Athene watched over the city of Athens.*

Why did the Greeks build temples?

Everywhere they settled, the Greeks built temples to honour their gods and goddesses. A temple usually had a statue of its own particular god inside. People came to the temple to bring gifts to the god and to pray for the god's help. Priests looked after the statue inside the temple.

Which Roman town disappeared under hot ash?

A Roman port called Pompeii in Italy – close to the foot of a volcano. In AD 79, the volcano, Vesuvius, suddenly erupted. Hot ashes, stones and cinders rained down on Pompeii. The layers of mud and ash preserved the Roman buildings so that today you can walk through the streets of the ruined city.

⬅ *Pompeii was only rediscovered in the 1700s. Archaeologists have now uncovered about 75 per cent of the city.*

Where is the Acropolis?

The Acropolis is a rocky platform on a hill in Athens, Greece. The term 'acropolis' means 'upper city'. Many of the cities of ancient Greece are built around an acropolis where the people can flee to in times of invasion, and the most sacred buildings are usually on an acropolis. Other Greek cities had an acropolis but Athens' is the most famous. The rock is about 350 m long and 150 m across. On top the Athenians built their royal palace and temples. The ruins of the most famous temple – the Parthenon – are still there.

History **highlights**

Greek and Roman **gods**

Greek	Roman	
Zeus	Jupiter	King of the gods
Ares	Mars	War
Artemis	Diana	Moon and hunting
Hera	Juno	Wife of Zeus
Athena	Minerva	Wisdom
Demeter	Ceres	Good harvests
Hades	Pluto	Underworld
Aphrodite	Venus	Love and beauty
Eros	Cupid	Love
Apollo	Apollo	Music and arts

Up **Pompeii**

Today, visitors to Pompeii walk into houses and down lanes, just as the Pompeiians did. In museums, they can see domestic items and the remains of people killed by the volcano. Volcanic ash hardened around victims' bodies, and formed a mould. As the bodies decayed, a shell was left. By filling the shells with plaster, archaeologists have made copies of the bodies.

➡ *Pompeii was destroyed when red-hot lava erupted from Vesuvius.*

Which Roman column tells stories?

Trajan's Column, which stands in Rome. It is a tall column of stone, erected in AD 113 to honour the Roman soldier-emperor Trajan. The column has a spiral staircase inside, and the outside is covered with carvings showing how the Roman army conquered Dacia (Romania and Hungary) under Trajan's command.

❷ *The relief carvings on Trajan's Column show us what Roman soldiers wore, and the equipment they used when going to war.*

Why did the Romans build aqueducts?

To allow towns access to fresh water. Roman engineers built pipes and arched bridges called aqueducts – raised channels that carried water from streams in mountains to cities. One of the most famous Roman aqueducts is the Pont du Gard, built in southern France about 2,000 years ago. It has three tiers, the topmost carrying water.

❶ *The Pont du Gard soars 47 m above the Gard River.*

How did the Colosseum get its name?

The Colossus of Rhodes, one of the Seven Wonders of the World, gave its name to anything gigantic. The Ancient Romans crowded the Colosseum, an oval amphitheatre seating 50,000 spectators. The huge seating area was divided into 80 sections, and had lifts and tunnels to let gladiators and wild animals into the arena. The Circus Maximus, a chariot race track in Rome, was even bigger, holding 250,000 people.

❶ *The Pantheon is a remarkable feat of engineering.*

Which Roman wonder had a hole in it?

One of the most remarkable buildings in ancient Rome was the Pantheon, a temple built during the rule of the emperor Hadrian (AD 117–138). The Pantheon was the largest circular building in the ancient world. It was topped by a dome measuring 43 m across. The dome had an opening in the top to let in light and air.

❶ *The mighty Colosseum in Rome was over 180 m long and 156 m across. It was supported by 80 arches.*

Key **dates**

Amazing **facts**

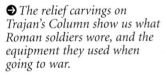

Five ways to get famous in Greece or Rome...
Be a successful gladiator
Be a top chariot racer
Win lots of battles
Be a philosopher
Be a star athlete

...or get killed
Be an unsuccessful gladiator
Lead a slave revolt
Fall off an aqueduct
Annoy the emperor
Holiday in Pompeii in AD 79

❶ *Gladiator fights were usually fights to the death.*

Amonument is any structure built in memory of a person or an event. It can be a statue of a king, a general or an explorer, a tower or column with names and words on it, or just an ancient heap of earth grown over with grass. National monuments can include historic buildings and even natural features, such as rocks.

⊕ *Stone circles often seem to be arranged so that they correspond with ancient annual festivals, such as the Summer Solstice.*

Where is the Great Serpent Mound?

In the woodland of Ohio, USA. It looks like a giant snake coiled round upon itself, but it is actually a mound of earth. Known as the Great Serpent Mound, it was created more than 2,000 years ago, and there are hundreds of other mounds like it. The mounds were piled up by Native American people across North America. Many were burial places, but the reasons for others remain a mystery. Monks Mound in the US state of Illinois is 30 m high and covers an area the size of ten soccer pitches! All the work to make it was was done by hand.

Why did ancient peoples build circles of stone?

It was probably for religious reasons. Some structures may have been used as calendars to mark the seasons – it is thought that ancient peoples could use the positions of the stones to help them fix dates by studying the Sun and stars. They could also have been used as giant maps, to show the direction of settlements. People met at these mysterious monuments for important ceremonies.

Ancient **monuments**

Circles and **mounds**

Stonehenge	England	Rings of cut stones	Built between 2950 and 1600 BC
Silbury Hill	England	Mound 40 m high	About 2100 BC
Carnac	France	3,000 stones	Dates vary; about 2000 BC
Avebury	England	Stone circles and earth banks	About 2000 BC

Amazing **facts**

STONEHENGE
Eighty 'bluestones' weighing up to 4 tonnes each were brought to Stonehenge from Wales, a distance of 385 km.

The biggest upright stones are 9 m long and weigh 50 tonnes; they came from 30 km away. Stonehenge may have been a temple, a meeting place or an astronomical observatory.

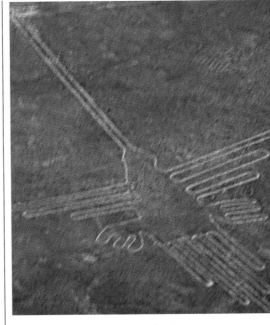

Which Pacific island has the strangest statues?

On lonely Easter Island, in the middle of the Pacific Ocean, stand more than 600 stone statues. Most look like heads peering out of the ground. The statues were made between AD 900 and 1600. Some weigh as much as 50 tonnes. Legend tells how the heads were made by people called 'Long Ears' who came in boats from South America.

⬆ *The Easter Island statues are a mystery. Why were they made? And why were so many statues later pushed over?*

Why does Stonehenge fascinate people?

Because no one is really certain about how it was built. Over two thousand years ago, people in Britain went to great efforts to construct a circle of stones. Stonehenge is the most famous of these strange circles. It was built in stages, from around 2800 BC, on Salisbury Plain. Using muscle power alone, the building of Stonehenge was an extremely daunting task. The stones are so heavy (some weigh as much as 50 tonnes) that dragging just one would have taken 500 men. The pairs of stones were once topped with cross-beam stones or lintels. Stonehenge was almost certainly built for the purpose of religious ceremonies, and would have been used as part of ancient rituals. The stones are one of England's most famous monuments.

⬅ *Local people once thought Stonehenge must have been built by the Devil.*

⬆ *The animal shapes made by the Nazca include a spider and a hummingbird. Some figures are over 120 m long.*

Where are there strange pictures in a desert?

In Peru, in South America. Why the Nazca people of Peru scraped lines in the desert to make long straight lines, geometric shapes and outlines of animals and birds is a mystery. The outlines are so big that they can only be seen properly from the air, and yet they were made centuries before people had balloons or aircraft. One theory suggests the Nazca made them over 1,500 years ago to trace the movements of the Sun and stars they saw in the sky above.

Stone Age temple?
At Avebury in Wiltshire, England, Stone Age builders dug into the chalk to make an enormous structure. They made a chalk bank 425 m across and 6 m high, and inside arranged a circle of 100 stone pillars (known as 'sarsens'), some weighing 50 tonnes. There were two smaller circles inside the big circle. Prehistoric Avebury may have been a temple and was probably built over 3,000 years ago.

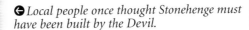

What were barrows?
A barrow was a prehistoric burial mound – a heap of earth covering the grave of a dead person. There are probably at least 40,000 in England alone. They come in different shapes: there are long barrows and round barrows. The round barrows are usually later in date. One Roman barrow, opened in Kent in the 1950s, had a folding iron chair inside.

⬅ *Round barrows usually only contain a single burial.*

For thousands of years, forts and castles have been strongholds for defence. The best place to build a fortress was usually on a hilltop, as this is the best position to see approaching attackers and because a hilltop is usually easiest to defend. Some medieval castles still tower above the surrounding landscape today.

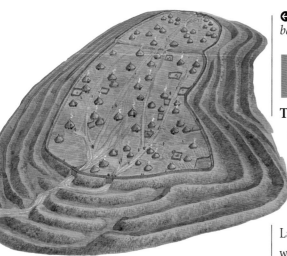

Maiden Castle was defended by ditches and banks, and by wooden fences and gates.

Krak des Chevaliers castle in Syria. It was built by Crusaders, but Muslims added extra defences after they captured it in 1271.

Who built Britain's strongest castles?

The Normans and the medieval kings of England who followed them. After the Norman Conquest, in 1066, Norman barons built stone motte and bailey castles: the motte was an earth mound, the bailey and the enclosure around it. Later, in the Middle Ages, when Edward I, who was king of England from 1272 to 1307, conquered Wales, he built huge stone castles to subdue the Welsh. Cannons brought an end to the age of castles in the 1400s.

What was Maiden Castle?

A hillfort, built by Iron Age people in Britain. Over 2,000 years ago these people, who were Celts, lived in groups or tribes. To protect themselves, and their farm animals, they built fortified villages on hilltops. Mai Dun or Maiden Castle in Dorset was one of the biggest hillforts ('Mai Dun' is Celtic for 'great hill'). It was captured by the Romans after they invaded Britain in AD 43. Some of its ramparts rise to a height of 6 m.

What is the Krak des Chevaliers?

A mighty Crusader castle. During the Crusades, or religious wars, of the Middle Ages, both sides (Muslims and Christians) built castles. Each side did its best to capture the enemy's castles, and castles often changed hands several times. The Crusader castle that is best-preserved is Krak des Chevaliers. It has very high walls on three sides and a moat on the fourth. It has a keep that is surrounded by a precipitous slope of smooth rock, and was known to the attacking Muslims as 'the Mountain' because it was impossible to climb.

Edward I's castles, such as Conwy Castle, were the wonders of their age.

Built to last

Strength in numbers

Earliest castle	Hattusas, Turkey	1500 BC
Oldest British castle	Richmond, Yorkshire, UK	1075
Biggest brick castle	Coca, Spain	1400s
Last of their line	Maginot Line forts, France	1930s

Roman forts
The Romans built small army forts to guard their frontiers. They also built legionary fortresses that were as big as small towns. They were smart too. Roman fort-builders made forts look stronger than they were, plastering over wooden walls to make them look like stone.

Enemies would think twice before attacking a Roman fort.

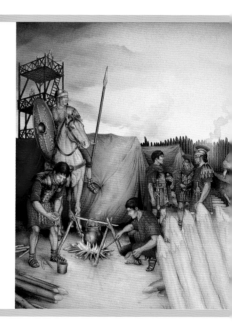

Where is the Red Fort?

In the Indian city of Delhi.
The Indian name for the fort is Lal Qal'ah, and the name comes from the reddish colour of its sandstone walls, which stand over 20 m high. The building of the Red Fort was begun in 1639 at the orders of the Mogul emperor of India, Shah Jahan. Within the walls there was space for Shah Jahan's royal palaces, gardens, soldiers' barracks, as well as all the important government buildings.

🔻 *Indian castles, such as the Red Fort in Delhi, often had bigger gateways than European castles – so that elephants could get through.*

Which castle sits on a volcano?

Edinburgh Castle, in Scotland. The volcano it is perched upon, known as Castle Rock, is extinct. There has been a settlement at Edinburgh since 850 BC. The city grew in the AD 1000s when David I established his court at Edinburgh Castle. David built a tiny chapel in the castle, dedicated to the memory of his mother, Margaret. The chapel is the oldest surviving structure on Castle Rock.

🔺 *Edinburgh Castle houses Mons Meg, a massive siege gun given to James II in 1457.*

🔺 *Great Zimbabwe was a trading city. Its walls measured up to 10 m high and 240 m long. Its stone walls protected the people and cattle inside.*

Where is Great Zimbabwe?

In Zimbabwe, in Central Africa. It is a fortified settlement, and one of the most impressive and famous ancient ruins in Africa. The walls of Great Zimbabwe are made of granite rock. Historians believe that the fort was built some time after AD 1000 by the Shona people: the word 'zimbabwe' means 'house of stone' in the Shona language. It is thought to have been built over a long period, beginning in 1200 and ending in 1450.

Amazing **facts**

- Many medieval castles had a flooded ditch or moat. The big square tower was called a keep. Outer 'curtain' walls were arranged in rings. Windows were like slits, for archers to shoot through.
- Some medieval castles had stone walls up to 7m thick.
- In India, castle doors sometimes had iron spikes to stop war elephants battering them open.
- Japanese castles had wooden walls filled in with clay and plaster. A cannon ball just went straight through.
- The longest siege was over 2,600 years ago, when the Egyptians besieged Ashdod (now in Israel) for 29 years.

Ways to capture a castle under siege…
Sit and wait for the people inside to starve, get sick or surrender
Climb ladders and siege towers to get over the walls
Blast holes in the walls with giant catapults hurling stones
Tunnel or mine beneath the walls
Smash down the gates with battering rams

…and ways to fight off the attackers
Shoot arrows from the battlements
Drop rocks on enemy soldiers
Pour hot water and hot oil on them
Set fire to wooden siege towers
Push away the ladders with poles

🔻 *Castles had to be well-protected, with many outer walls.*

Kings and emperors built palaces to show how rich and powerful they were. Today, some palaces are museums. Power has shifted to elected assemblies, such as parliaments, but even some presidents still live in palaces. The biggest palace in China and the most luxurious palaces of modern times were built for the homes of the rulers of oil-rich kingdoms such as Saudi Arabia and Brunei.

⬆ *China's finest artists worked to decorate the Forbidden City. Construction started in 1406 and took 14 years to complete. An estimated one million workers were involved.*

How old is Buckingham Palace?

The bit that most tourists see and photograph, the front, dates from 1913. So Buckingham Palace is a fairly new palace, as palaces go. It was originally Buckingham House, a mansion bought by King George III in the 1700s. From 1837 it was the London home of Queen Victoria, and ever since has been the London home of the king or queen.

⬇ *Although in use for the many official events held by the Queen, areas of Buckingham Palace are open to visitors.*

Which palace was built for a general?

Not all palaces were homes for kings and queens. Blenheim Palace in England was built (1705–25) for the Duke of Marlborough. He was England's most famous soldier. The huge house was a thank-you from Queen Anne and her government for Marlborough's victories against the French. It is named after one of his victories at the Battle of Blenheim. Later, Blenheim Palace was the birthplace of another famous Englishman, Winston Churchill.

Who lived in the Forbidden City?

Chinese emperors, with their families. Palaces were centres of government as well as luxurious homes. Some were cities built in miniature, like the Imperial Palace in Beijing, China. It was designed for the Ming emperors, and work on building it began in 1406. The job took a million workers ten years. The emperor and his family lived in the most secret part, known as the Forbidden City, because no foreigners were ever allowed to enter. The Forbidden City is now open to the public as a palace museum.

Fit for a **king**

Most famous power **houses**

10 Downing Street – London home of the British prime minister
Elysee Palace – Paris home of the French president
White House, Washington DC – home of the president of the United States
Kremlin, Moscow – seat of government power in Russia
General Assembly Building, New York – headquarters of the United Nations
Berlaymont, Brussels – centre of power of the European Union

Lost **room**

The Amber Room in the Summer Palace at St Petersburg was decorated with 12 tonnes of amber. A gift from the King of Prussia in 1716, the room disappeared during World War II (1939–45). A replica was created to replace it.

➡ *The Summer Palace at St Petersburg.*

世界人民大团结万

Which king ordered a palace with 1,300 rooms?

King Louis XIV of France in the 1600s. Louis had big ideas and he wanted a bigger palace than any other king. In 1661 work began on his new palace at Versailles, outside Paris. It had to be big – Louis's court had 20,000 people, and Versailles became the centre of court life.

⬆ *The Palace of Versailles is now a museum.*

Who was the first president to live in the White House?

The first president to live there was John Adams. The White House, in Washington, DC, is one of the world's most recognized buildings. It is the home of the president of the United States. The original house was built in the 1790s. It was burnt down in 1814, and rebuilt. Various presidents have made changes to it over the years. The White House has 132 rooms, including the president's Oval Office.

⊘ *St Petersburg was founded by Tsar Peter the Great in 1703 to be his new capital (instead of Moscow).*

Where is the Winter Palace?

In St Petersburg, Russia. This area is so far north, close to the Baltic Sea, that in winter, days are very short. The Winter Palace was built in 1754–62 as a winter home for the royal family – another palace outside the city served as their summer home. The Russian tsars wanted the Winter Palace to rival any royal building in western Europe. Russia no longer has a tsar and the Winter Palace is now an art museum, called the Hermitage, with one of the world's great art collections – there are nearly three million works on exhibit.

Did You **know?**

After Whitehall Palace burned down in 1619, a new palace was planned but only the Banqueting House was built. Charles I was beheaded outside it in 1649.

The medieval Palace of Westminster was home to English kings and queens. Today, only Westminster Hall survives.

The Westminster Parliament escaped being blown up by Guy Fawkes in 1605, but was burned down in 1834.

⊘ *King Charles I quarrelled so badly with Parliament about religion and taxes that he provoked a civil war that resulted in his execution.*

Amazing **palaces**

Sacred Palace, Constantinople (modern Istanbul) – covered an area bigger than 50 football pitches.

Doge's Palace – elegant home of the ruler or doge of Venice.

Pitti Palace – in Florence, Italy, built by the Pitti family in the 1400s and now an art museum.

Whitehall – London, a Tudor palace where Henry VIII died in 1547, burned down in 1619.

Escorial – Spain's most famous palace, built for the gloomy King Philip II as a monastery and library with many valuable old books.

A wall is built to keep people in or out. Towers can be part of a wall. One of the most mysterious walls is a 160 km-long earth bank known as the Eredo in Nigeria. It is partially hidden by dense forest, and is thought to be about 1,000 years old but no one is certain why it is there.

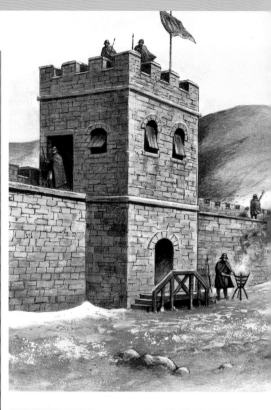

⬆ *The Great Wall is the longest structure ever built, but in the end it did not keep out invaders.*

Why did the Chinese build the Great Wall?

The Great Wall of China was built to protect China against 'barbarian' invaders from the north. Chinese civilization was based on farming, and the young Chinese nation was often raided by nomads from the North. In the 200s BC, the Chinese emperor Shi Huangdi ordered old frontier walls to be linked by walls and forts to keep its nusiance neighbours out. The Great Wall winds for more than 6,400 km over mountains, hills and plateaus and along the edges of deserts. The wall was 9 m high, and was originally dotted with watchtowers with a walkway along the top for patrolling guards. Some sections of the Great Wall are now in ruins or have even disappeared, but it is still one of the world's most momentous sights.

Which was the longest Roman wall?

Hadrian's Wall (named after the Emperor Hadrian) stretches for 118 km across the hills of northern England from Wallsend-on-Tyne in the east to Bowness on the Solway Firth in the west. In the AD 120s, Roman legionary soldiers built this wall to control travel between Roman Britain and the north, and to keep out northern tribes. When it was first built, the wall was 2 to 3 m thick and 117 km in length. Long stretches of the wall still wind over the hills.

Dizzying **heights**

Amazing **facts**

- Though no longer the tallest skyscraper, the Sears Tower in Chicago, USA (443 m) still has the most floors: 110.

- The first skyscraper was built by Le Baron Jenney in Chicago, 1885. It had just ten floors.

- The Empire State Building, New York City, is probably the world's most recognized tall building; built in 1931 it is 381 m high.

↩ *The Ananda Temple in Myanma, Burma, was completed in 1091. It rises in graduated terraces to a height of 52 m.*

↑ *Hadrian's wall was defended by ditches. At every Roman mile (1500 m) there was a mini fort with a tower to guard crossing points.*

Why is the Eiffel Tower so remarkable?

People laughed when Gustave Eiffel said he planned to built a steel tower over 300 m high in Paris. But he did. The Eiffel Tower was built in two years, 1887–89, to celebrate the 100th anniversary of the French Revolution. It was assembled from 12,000 sections, held together by over two million rivets.

⬇ *For 40 years, the Eiffel Tower was the tallest structure in the world. It is still the most famous landmark in France.*

What made the Tower of Pisa lean?

Tall buildings are heavy, as medieval builders of Pisa, in Italy, soon discovered. In the 1150s, the city's new bell-tower began to tilt before it was half finished. The soil underneath was just too soft. Even when the tower was finished, in the 1300s, it leaned perilously. Modern engineers have worked hard to make sure that its lean does not turn into a collapse! The Leaning Tower is 56 m high and one of Italy's most popular tourist attractions.

Where are the Petronas Towers?

In Malaysia, where they are a national symbol. The USA was the first country to build skyscrapers in the 1800s, but countries all over the world have competed to build taller skyscrapers. In 1996 the twin Petronas Towers rose high above the city of Kuala Lumpur and Malaysia was number one in the skyscraper charts. The towers are 452 m high, and house 88 storeys of offices.

Above the **clouds**

In the Middle Ages, the tallest buildings were church spires and campaniles (bell-towers). Sometimes cathedral builders aimed too high and towers fell down. The main spire of Lincoln Cathedral in England was the highest in the world (160 m) until 1548, when it collapsed. Each of its three towers had spires – today there are none.

Extreme **measures**

Longest wall	The Great Wall of China
Tallest tower	CN Tower in Canada 555 m high
Most famous seaside tower	Blackpool, England
Longest Roman wall	Hadrian's Wall, northern Britain
Most topsy-turvy tower	Leaning Tower of Pisa, Italy
Biggest pagoda	Shwe Dagon pagoda, Burma
Most gloomy tower	Bloody Tower in the Tower of London
Noisiest tower	The legendary Tower of Babel

↶ *Architects have speculated as to whether the top-most storey of the leaning tower should be removed, in an effort to stabilize it.*

Some inspiring and very large buildings have been erected for religious worship. Often, as with medieval cathedrals in Europe, construction took many years. Sometimes, the same building has served two faiths – Hagia Sophia in Constantinople (now Istanbul) was built as a Christian church, but later became a Muslim mosque. It is now a museum.

❶ *Buddhism spread from India across Southeast Asia to the islands of Indonesia. Borobudur is on the island of Java.*

What are the world's biggest religious buildings?

The world's biggest Christian church is St Peter's in Rome (1506–1614). But bigger still is the Hindu temple-city of Angkor Wat. Built by the Khmer people of Cambodia in the 1100s, its moated enclosure measures 1,500 by 1,400 m, and it has five central towers, the tallest 70 m high. The moat around Angkor Wat measures 6 km. The temple was abandoned in the 1400s.

Where can 300,000 people pray together?

In a mosque. It is where followers of Islam (Muslims) gather for prayers. The biggest Muslim mosque is the Shah Faisal Mosque in Islamabad, Pakistan. Inside its courtyard, 40,000 people can worship. The building is named after a ruler of Saudi Arabia who helped pay for its construction. It is situated on the outskirts of Pakistan's capital city, Islamabad, which means 'place of Islam'.

Which temple has 500 Buddhas?

The biggest Buddhist temple is Borobudur in Java, Indonesia. Built in the AD 700s, it fell into disuse about 1000 years ago, but was restored in the early 1900s. It was built by shaping a small hill and casing it with stone blocks. The Borobudur temple has 500 images of Buddha (Siddhartha Gautama) and thousands of other sculptures. The decoration shows links with Persian, Babylonian and Greek styles. Since 1972 all of the temple's 800,000 stones have been taken away, cleaned and replaced.

❷ *Angkor Wat rises from the jungle, which for centuries has threatened to completely engulf it.*

Biggest temple

The biggest temple ever built was the Temple of Amun at Karnak in Egypt. It was erected in about 1250 BC. However, hardly anyone walked through its vast halls or had access to the building. Only a few priests were allowed inside. Its massive courts and pillared halls were bigger than Angkor Wat.

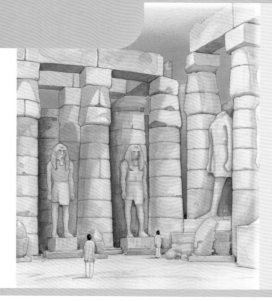

Sometimes cathedral builders aimed too high! The main spire of Lincoln Cathedral in England was the highest in the world (160 m) until 1548, when it collapsed. Each of its three towers had spires – today there are none.

❸ *Visitors can still see the remains of the Temple of Amun in Egypt.*

❸ *The statue of Christ the Redeemer above Rio de Janeiro, Brazil.*

What is the Taj Mahal?

The Taj Mahal is a tomb, built for Mumtaz Mahal, wife of the Mogul emperor of India, Shah Jahan. When she died in 1629, her husband ordered a special tomb to be built for her. It took 20,000 workers 20 years to complete the white marble building with its graceful minarets (towers). Under the white marble dome, which is 60-m-high, the emperor and his wife are buried together.

● *The Taj Mahal, located near the city of Agra in India, is considered to be one of the world's greatest architectural treasures.*

⬆ *St Paul's Cathedral survived bombs during the Blitz in World War II (1939–45).*

Which is Britain's most famous cathedral?

Probably St Paul's Cathedral in London. Sir Christopher Wren's building (1675–1710) replaced a medieval cathedral burned down in the Great Fire of 1666. However, it has rivals, such as Westminster Abbey, begun by Edward the Confessor in the 1040s, and York Minster, England's biggest medieval cathedral. Many people also visit Canterbury Cathedral, which dates from the 1070s, and Salisbury Cathedral, which has the tallest spire in England at 123 m. The world's biggest cathedral (though not the biggest church) is the medieval-style Cathedral of St John the Divine, which is in New York City.

Amazing **facts**

Longest cathedral nave: St John the Divine, New York City – 183 m

Britain's largest cathedral: Liverpool's Cathedral Church of Christ

Church with most statues: Chartres Cathedral, France – 10,000

Tallest cathedral spire: Ulm cathedral, Germany – 161 m

Tallest minaret: Hassan II Mosque, Morocco – 176 m

Highest spire in Britain: Salisbury Cathedral – 123 m

Biggest Jewish synagogue: New York City

➡ *Ulm Cathedral was begun in 1377 but the immense stone tower at its western end was not completed until 1890.*

Technology – the application of science – has changed our lives amazingly. We can send space probes deep into space and take pictures with a mobile telephone. In the early 1800s, before the first steam train or camera had been invented, people would have regarded such marvels as fantasy – or magic.

⬆ *Thrust SSC was designed to keep its wheels on the ground – and not become a flying car!*

What were the biggest airships of all time?

The biggest flying machines in the 1930s were two German airships. They were called the *Hindenburg* and *Graf Zeppelin*. At 245 m, they were longer than passenger jets are today. Powered by propellers, the airships cruised at around 130km/h across the oceans. The loss of the *Hindenburg*, which exploded in 1937, brought the age of passenger airships to an end.

Which car went supersonic?

In 1997 Andy Green (GB) drove the British jet Thrust SSC car across the flat sands of the Black Rock Desert in Nevada in the USA. He travelled at a speed faster than sound. His top speed of 1,227.985 km/h became a new land speed record. The car featured two Rolls-Royce Spey 205 jet engines, and it travelled faster than a jet airliner. The Thrust SSC also reached speeds more than three times faster than the fastest conventional-engined car – a 1998 McLaren F-1.

How do scientists explore distant worlds?

By studying the Universe with telescopes on the ground, and by sending telescopes into orbit around the Earth and spacecraft on journeys across the Solar System. In January 2004, scientists watched pictures of the planet Mars taken by NASA's Spirit rover. Robots make good space explorers. Astronauts need food, water and air. Robots just need energy, so they can keep sending back data. Mars Pathfinder carried a small rover called *Sojourner* to Mars in 1997. It was only about the size of a microwave oven.

⬇ *Robot explorers can trundle around millions of kilometres from Earth, beaming back pictures of Mars.*

Record **firsts**

Key **dates**

1769	Steam carriage
1783	Balloon flight
1807	Steamship
1830	Steam railway
1879	Electric train
1885	Motor car
1903	Flight in an aeroplane
1939	Jet plane
1957	Satellite in Earth orbit
1969	Moon landing by humans

⬆ *In 1957 the Russians launched Sputnik 1, the first satellite.*

Land speed **records**

1899	Jenatzy's La Jamais *Contente*	106 km/h
1907	Stanley steam car	241 km/h
1927	Henry Segrave's *Sunbeam*	328 km/h
1932	Malcom Campbell's *Bluebird*	408 km/h
1947	John Cobb's *Railton Special*	634 km/h
1964	Craig Breedlove's *Spirit of America*	846 km/h
1970	Gary Gabelich's *Blue Flame*	1,016 km/h
1983	Richard Noble's *Thrust 2*	1,019 km/h
1997	Andy Green's *Thrust SSC*	1,227 km/h

Which is the world's fastest train?

The French TGV – a high-speed train that normally travels at around 300 km/h but in 1990 sped along at a world record speed of 515 km/h. It set the world speed record on a national rail system between Courtalain and Tours. Modern high-speed trains are five times faster than the first steam trains of the 1830s. The fastest speed reached by a steam train was 202.73 km/h by the British LNER locomotive *Mallard* in 1938. Maglev trains are exceptionally fast, as they are suspended by powerful magnets above a guide track. Early versions were built in Germany and Japan, and in 1996 a maglev train started operating at Disney World in Florida, USA. In 2002, a German-built maglev train in Shanghai, China topped 430 km/h.

Which were the biggest vehicles ever?

The biggest vehicles ever made were two Marion crawlers, giant tractors used by the US space agency NASA to move rockets and space shuttles into position for launching. The crawlers have eight caterpillar tracks and when loaded each weighs 8,000 tonnes – about 15 times heavier than the biggest dumper trucks (over 500 tonnes). They were developed to carry an assembled Saturn rocket on its 5-mile journey from the assembly building to the launching pad.

⊕ *High-speed trains run on special express routes across Europe, North America and Japan.*

⊕ Great Eastern *was not a success as a passenger ship, but it did lay a telegraph cable across the Atlantic Ocean.*

Which was the most wondrous ship of its day?

The *Great Eastern* was a giant in its day (1858). Over 19,000 tonnes and 211 m long, it was bigger than any ship built in the next 40 years. Designed by British engineer Isambard Kingdom Brunel, *Great Eastern* was the only ship to have screw propellers driven by its steam engines, but it also had paddle-wheels for extra power and a full set of sails.

⊕ *The biggest and strongest steam locomotives ever were designed to haul 3,000-tonne freight trains over the Rocky Mountains.*

Amazing **facts**

- The biggest locomotive was the steam-powered *Big Boy* loco (USA) in 1941.
- The heaviest aircraft to lumber off the ground is a Russian Antonov An-225, 600 tonnes.
- The world's longest car was a US freaky vehicle with built-in swimming pool: 30.5 m long, with 26 wheels.
- The largest ship ever built was the tanker *Jahre Viking*, 564,763 tonnes and 458 m long.
- The world's biggest cruise liner was *Queen Mary 2*, 345 m long, 150,000 tonnes and as high as a 23-storey building.
- The heaviest load into space was the 5,600-kg Cassini-Huygens probe, launched by a Titan IV rocket in 1997.

Engineering puts scientific knowledge to practical use. While the construction of the Egyptian pyramids was one of the greatest engineering feats of ancient times, today there is no end to the marvels that engineering can offer – a bridge soaring high above water, a tunnel beneath the ocean and a telescope orbiting in space.

Which telescope orbits our planet?

The Space Telescope. Telescopes on the Earth get only a murky view of the stars, because the atmosphere (the air around the planet) gets in the way. The Hubble Space Telescope was launched into orbit in 1990 to give astronomers a clearer look at the Universe. It circles the Earth at a height of about 600 km, and from above the atmosphere it can observe objects 50 times fainter than Earth telescopes can see.

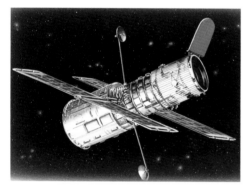

⬆ *The Space Telescope is named after the American astronomer Edwin Hubble (1889–1953) who made important discoveries about galaxies (star clusters).*

⬆ *Suspension bridges such as the Akashi Kaikyo Bridge in Japan can carry road or rail traffic. The weight of the bridge is hung (suspended) between the tall towers.*

How are very long bridges held up?

The world's longest bridges are suspension bridges, held up by wire cables slung between high towers. The Akashi Kaikyo Bridge links Japan's main island, Honshu, with the neighbouring island of Shikoku. The bridge spans 2 km of sea – the longest road bridge in the world.

⬆ *The white cladding on the shells of the Sydney Opera House is built from one million ceramic tiles.*

Which is Australia's most famous building?

The Sydney Opera House (1973) is Australia's most famous building. Danish architect Joern Utzon designed its futuristic look – the materials needed for the roofs had not been invented when work began in 1959. The white shell roof structures are thought to echo the shape of the sails of the boats in the harbour, and beneath them are theatres and performance halls.

Great dams

People moved by giant dam

The Three Gorges dam project in China will not be completed for several years. It involves building the world's biggest dam to hold back the waters of the Yangtze River, creating a lake 600 km long. Some 500 towns and villages will disappear under water, and one million people will be moved to new homes.

Rogun Dam in Tajikistan is the world's highest dam. It is 335 m high. It is a large rock and earth-filled dam on the Vakhsh River in southern Tajikistan, upstream from the Nurek Dam.

Amazing facts

LONGEST SUSPENSION BRIDGES

Name	Country	Span
Akashi Kaikyo	Japan	1,991 m
Great Belt	Denmark	1,624 m
Humber	Britain	1,410 m
Jianyin	China	1,385 m
Tsing Ma	China	1,377 m

⬇ *The Akosombo Dam was built in the 1960s, to supply electricity to Ghana and neighbouring countries.*

Where can you sail through a desert?

When ships use the Suez Canal, to travel between the Mediterranean and Red seas, the dry desert lands of Egypt lies on either bank. When a canal was first suggested, critics said the hot sun would dry up the water. The Suez Canal was opened in 1869, shortening the sea route between Britain and India by almost 10,000 km. The canal is about 180 km long, around 225 m wide at the surface (it gets narrower as it nears the bottom) and 20 m deep.

Where do trains travel under the sea?

Trains speed through the Channel Tunnel (Eurotunnel) under the sea between Britain and France. There are three tunnels: two rail tunnels and a smaller service tunnel, running for over 14 km under the sea and 30 km underground. The idea of a Channel tunnel was first suggested in the 1800s, but it was not until 1994 that the first high-speed trains began using Eurotunnel.

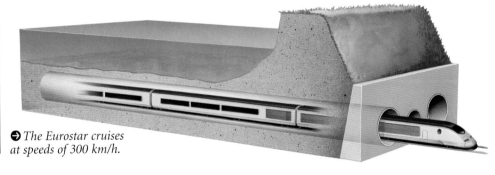

➡ *The Eurostar cruises at speeds of 300 km/h.*

Which dam made the biggest lake?

The biggest artificial lake is Lake Volta in Ghana, west Africa. When a dam is built across a river, the water held up behind the barrier forms a lake. This water can then be used for irrigation or to drive hydro-electric turbines. Lake Volta has an area of more than 8,000 sq km, but it is still small compared to North America's biggest Great Lake, Lake Superior (82,000 sq km).

⬇ *One of the most ambitious projects of the 21st century is to develop the orbital Space Station, and then launch manned missions to Mars and other planets.*

Dams and **bridges**

Aswan High Dam – Built across the Nile in Egypt and completed 1970

Sydney Harbour Bridge – landmark arch bridge in Sydney, Australia, opened 1932

Tower Bridge – London's most famous bridge, opened 1894

Brooklyn Bridge – Famous early suspension bridge, opened in 1894

➡ *The middle of Tower Bridge can be raised to permit large vessels to pass.*

Memorials help us remember events or people. Some memorials are so big that it's impossible to miss them. But others are hidden. Sometimes, treasures found in the ground reveal hidden stories about a long-lost past.

What was unearthed at Sutton Hoo?

A king who ruled East Anglia in England in the 600s. He was buried in a wooden ship, 27 m long. The ship had been placed in a trench, and inside lay the body of a warrior, probably a powerful local king called Raedwald of the East Angles. He had been buried with clothes, weapons and treasure. Then his ship-grave had been filled in. The ship-burial remained undiscovered until unearthed by archaeologists at Sutton Hoo in Suffolk in 1939.

A replica of the Sutton Hoo helmet, found in the ship-burial.

The Gateway Arch is the tallest monument in the USA. It was completed in 1965.

Whose journey is remembered by a giant arch?

American pioneers. The Gateway to the West in St Louis, USA is an192-m U-shaped arch that stands beside the Mississippi River. It commemorates the migration of thousands of settlers who set off in wagon trains to make new homes in the West in the 1840s–1870s.

Who was buried with an army of clay soldiers?

The Chinese emperor, Shih Huang-di, in around 210 BC. The ancient Chinese believed their dead rulers would need servants and soldiers in the after-life. So when Shi Huang-di, the first Qin emperor, died his tomb was filled with clay models of soldiers. Archaeologists were amazed to find them in 1974 when part of the huge imperial tomb complex was opened.

The terracotta clay warriors of the Chinese emperor's immortal army.

Ancient **treasures**

What's wonderful about a mummy?

The Egyptians believed in life after death and made careful preparations for death and burial. They believed it was important to preserve the body of a dead person. The body was treated with chemicals and oils and then dried, to stop it decaying. The mummy was wrapped in linen bandages and put in a coffin, inside a tomb, along with clothes, weapons, jewels and food.

When ready for burial, a mummy was placed inside a special coffin. Some of these were shaped and richly decorated.

Famous **monuments**

The highest column in the world commemorates the battle of San Jacinto, fought between Texans and Mexicans in 1836. Britain's famous monuments include The Monument (a column marking the spot in London where the Great Fire of 1666 began) and Nelson's Column in Trafalgar Square in London, with a statue of Admiral Horatio Nelson on top.

Whose tomb revealed a lost treasure?

Tutankhamun, who became king of Egypt about 1347 BC but died aged 18. He was buried in the Valley of the Kings. In 1922, his tomb was found by the British archaeologist Howard Carter. Inside were astonishing treasures – more than 5,000 objects including chests, necklaces, chariots, swords, ostrich feathers, models of ships, toys and jars of precious oils.

⊕ *Among the finds in Tutankhamun's tomb was the gold death mask of the young king.*

⊕ *The Spaniards never found the Inca fortress of Machu Picchu. Today, half a million tourists visit it every year.*

Which leaders stare out from a mountain?

Four US presidents, whose stone heads loom from rocky Mount Rushmore in South Dakota, USA. Carving work began in 1927. It took four years to build and cost $1 million. Each head is as big as a five-storey building and the faces tower 1,800 m above sea level. The carvings are scaled to men who would stand 141 m tall. On each carving, the president's nose is 6 m long, the mouth 5 m wide and the eyes are 3 m across. The Mount Rushmore National Memorial honours four of the most important US Presidents – these are George Washington, Thomas Jefferson, Theodore Roosevelt and Abraham Lincoln.

Where did the last Incas live in secret?

High in the Andes, at Machu Picchu and other strongholds. The Spaniards conquered the Inca civilization in the 1500s, but never managed to capture the Incas' last stronghold. The ruins of the walled Inca city of Machu Picchu lie in the mountains near Cuzco in Peru. Machu Picchu remained unknown to the world until discovered by an American explorer, Hiram Bingham, in 1911. The local people called it 'Machu Picchu', meaning 'old mountain'.

Mighty **monuments**

Name	Where	Height
Gateway to the West	St Louis, USA	192 m
San Jacinto Monument	Texas, USA	173 m
Washington Monument	Washington DC, USA	169 m
Motherland statue	Russia	82 m
The Monument	London, UK	61 m
Nelson's Column	London, UK	51 m

Famous **treasure**

Tutankhamen's tomb – opened by Howard Carter in 1922 and found to still contain most of its original tomb-treasures.

Inca loot – In 1532 the Spanish conquistador Pizarro demanded a huge ransom for the Inca leader Atahualpa – a roomful of gold, and another filled with silver. The Incas paid, but the Spaniards still killed Atahualpa. They melted down the treasures to make gold and silver bars.

Pirate treasure – Captain Kidd and other pirates may have hidden treasure on lonely islands, but wrecked ships are the best places to search!

⊕ *Treasure divers still hunt for wrecks of ships lost in storms around Britain in 1588 and thought to be carrying Spanish gold.*

Natural landscapes are true wonders of the world. Mountains form great chains, or ranges, such as the Andes and Rocky mountains. There are great lakes, mighty rivers, grinding glaciers, seas so salty no one can sink and ice sheets so thick you could bury several office blocks beneath them!

❶ *Snow-capped Himalayan peaks in Nepal provide a dramatic view.*

Where are the world's mightiest mountains?

The highest mountains in the world are the Himalaya–Karakoram range in Asia. This great range has the world's top 20 peaks, all over 8,000 m high, and includes the world's highest peak, Mount Everest. The Himalayas are also one of the youngest mountain belts, as they were formed within the last 50 million years. The highest range of mountains in the western hemisphere is the Andes, which has more than 50 peaks that top 6,000 m.

Which is the strangest lake?

Probably the Dead Sea, which is actually a lake about nine times saltier than the oceans, such as the Pacific. The Dead Sea is in the Middle East, and is entirely surrounded by hot desert. The heat makes the seawater evaporate, leaving behind a high concentration of salt. Because of this, a bather can float in the water with no effort.

Where is the thickest ice?

In Antarctica, where the thickest ice is 4,800 m deep – more than ten times the height of the tallest building in the world. Antarctica is much bigger than Europe or Australia, but this is mainly because of the vast area of ice that covers the rock beneath. Situated at the southernmost tip of the Earth, it is large and mountainous. Antarctica is even colder than the Arctic and very dangerous. It has about 90 per cent of all the ice on the planet and is the windiest and driest of the continents. Antarctica was first explored by man less than 200 years ago, because the extremes of temperature were so great, yet millions of years ago it was ice-free and animals roamed there.

❶ *Antarctica is the only continent with no permanent human population and no trees.*

Biggest and **best**

Greatest depths

Oceans	Area (million sq km)	Greatest depth (m)
Pacific	166.2	10,924
Atlantic	86.6	9,460
Indian	74	7,542

Ocean facts

Deepest	Pacific Ocean
Shallowest	Atlantic Ocean
Coldest	Arctic Ocean

Highest **peaks**

Mount Olympus – The highest mountain in Greece: ancient Greeks believed Olympus was the home of the gods.
The Matterhorn – A mountain in the Alps (Switzerland–Italy, 4,478 m) first climbed by British mountaineer Edward Whymper in 1865.
Mount Fuji – In Japan, many people believe that Mount Fuji, the highest mountain in Japan, is a holy mountain.

❷ *Mount Fuji was formed by a volcano that last erupted in 1707.*

Where is Monument Valley?

In the state of Utah in the USA. Here, red sandstone rocks rise up from the desert, looking like towers and castles. The rocks are hundreds of millions of years old, and the 'monuments' have been shaped by weathering by wind, rain, frost and sun.

Where are there too many trees to count?

In the Amazon rainforest of South America, which has more trees of varying species than anywhere else. Tropical rainforests have about ten times as many tree species in a typical area than a cool-climate forest. Where you might find ten trees in a European forest, you might find 100 in the Amazon. Unfortunately the Amazon has been very badly damaged by 'deforestation' (logging) in recent years.

↟ *The lush tropical jungle of the Amazon remains one of the greatest natural wonders.*

↑ *Monument Valley is a favourite location for film-makers because of its spectacular scenery.*

Which is the world's biggest desert?

The Sahara in Africa, which has an area of over 9 million sq km. It covers much of northern Africa. The continent with the most deserts is Asia – it has four. Most of the Sahara is gravel, but in the sandy areas huge wave-like hummocks, or dunes, are pushed along by the wind. Cave paintings found near the region, drawn by ancient people, depict grassland animals. This shows that thousands of years ago the Sahara was wetter, with lakes and plains.

↑ *In parts of the Sahara there are sand dunes over 400 m high.*

Biggest **deserts**

Sahara – 9 million sq km in northern Africa
Australian – 1.5 million sq km in central Australia
Arabian – 1.3 million sq km in Saudi Arabia and Yemen
Gobi – 1 million sq km in Mongolia and China
Kalahari – 520,000 sq km in southern Africa

Longest **rivers**

Name	Location	Length (km)
Nile	Africa	6,670
Amazon	South America	6,448
Mississippi	Missouri, USA	5,970
Yenisey	Asia	5,540
Chang Jiang	Asia	5,530

Planet Earth is the only planet in our Solar System with such a staggering variety of stupendous sights, from vast canyons to thundering waterfalls. Many of these natural wonders have been here for far longer than human-beings. Most have taken millions of years to gradually evolve to how they are today.

⬆ *The Angel Falls in South America.*

⬆ *The rocks of the Grand Canyon change colour as the light changes during the day.*

What makes the Grand Canyon so grand?

The Grand Canyon in the United States is the largest gorge in the world. The canyon is an enormous winding gash, about 446 km long and from 1.6 to 29 km wide. It is getting deeper still, as the waters of the Colorado River continue to gradually cut away the rocks. Some rocks in the Grand Canyon are two billion years old.

Which waterfall is higher than a skyscraper?

Angel Falls in Venezuela is the highest waterfall in the world. Angel Falls has a total height of 979 m and its longest unbroken drop is 807 m. They are named after Jimmy Angel, an American pilot, who saw the spectacular Falls when he flew over them in 1935 while searching for gold.

Extraordinary Earth

Highest waterfalls

Angel	Venezuela	979 m
Tugela	South Africa	947 m
Utigard	Norway	800 m

Famous waterfalls

The world's best-known waterfalls are the Victoria Falls in Africa, and Niagara Falls, shared between Canada and the USA. Over the Victoria Falls, the Zambezi River, about 1.6 km wide, drops 108 m into a gigantic gorge. The local name of the Falls is Mosi oa Tunya (smoke that thunders), because of the roar and the clouds of spray.

Niagara Falls is two waterfalls: the Horseshoe Falls in Canada (51 m high and 792 m wide) and the American Falls in the USA (54 m high and 305 m wide).

⬆ *Uluru glows orange-red with reflected light at sunrise and sunset. The rock has lots of small caves, many of which are covered with Aboriginal paintings.*

Which is America's most destructive volcano?

Mount St Helens, a volcano in the Cascade Mountains, Washington state, on the west coast. It has erupted many times in its ancient history, and in 1980 it blew its top violently. Shaken by an earthquake measuring 5.1 on the Richter scale, the north face of this tall symmetrical mountain collapsed in a massive rock debris avalanche. The explosion blew off the peak's top, and sent hot ash and smoke high into the air. The forest caught fire, melting snow caused landslides, and millions of trees were instantly flattened. Nearly 78 sq km of forest was blown over or was left dead but still standing, and 57 people were killed. The eruption lasted nine hours, but Mount St Helens and the surrounding landscape were dramatically changed within moments. Scientists expect Mount St Helens to erupt again in the future, but cannot predict exactly when it might happen.

Which is Australia's biggest pebble?

Uluru or Ayers Rock in Australia. This massive loaf-shaped block of sandstone, more than 480 million years old, lies in the Northern Territory and is 348 m high, over 2.4 km long and 1.6 km wide. The aboriginal name for the rock, now commonly used, is Uluru and means 'great pebble'. The rock is a sacred aboriginal site.

Which is the longest coral reef?

The Great Barrier Reef in Australia, which stretches for about 2,010 km along the northeast coast of Australia. A coral reef is a limestone formation made of the hardened skeletons of dead water animals called polyps. Billions of living polyps are attached to the reef. Most of the Great Barrier Reef is a national park, and an ideal environment for about 1,500 kinds of fish, crabs, giant clams, sea turtles and birds.

⬇ *Scientists believe the Great Barrier Reef began to form about 30 million years ago.*

Dangerous **volcanoes**

- Etna on the island of Sicily, Italy; rumbles a lot
- Vesuvius, overlooks Bay of Naples, Italy and destroyed Pompeii
- Mt Pelée, Martinique; the 1902 eruption killed 38,000 people
- Krakatau in Indonesia, erupted in 1883; noise was heard 4,800 km away
- Mount St Helens in Washington, USA; erupted violently in 1980
- Mauna Loa, Hawaii, USA; world's biggest volcano, 9,100 m from Pacific seabed to peak

⬅ *Originally over two trillion litres of water an hour flowed over the edge of Niagara Falls. Half of this volume is now diverted for hydro-electric power by the governments of the United States and Canada.*

Nature's record-breakers come in all shapes and sizes, from tiny insects to enormous trees. Many animals can perform incredible feats of strength, speed and endurance. No human athlete could compete with the top animal record-breakers.

➔ *Termites are sometimes called white ants, but they are not related to ants.*

⬆ *The cheetah has long legs and at full speed its back arches for extra power.*

Which is the fastest land animal?

Cheetahs are the world's fastest land animals and can move as fast as a car. Within two seconds of starting a chase a cheetah may be running at 75 km/h, and it soon reaches a top speed of about 105 km/h. Cheetahs run out of energy after only 30 seconds of sprinting, so if an antelope can keep out of the cheetah's jaws for this short time, it may escape. Cheetahs do not often climb trees as they have difficulty in getting down again. They prefer wide open spaces, where they can easily spot prey, such as gazelles and hares.

Where is the most massive tree?

The heaviest tree is a giant sequoia or 'big tree' called General Sherman, growing in Sequoia National Park, California, USA. This forest giant can reach up to 84 m high and has an average measurement of 31.4 m round its trunk. It weighs about 2,500 tonnes – as much as 350 elephants. The giant redwood is the tallest tree, growing up to 113 m tall. They can live for over a thousand years – one redwood in California is 2,200 years old.

➔ *Giant redwood trees grow even taller than sequoias, but their trunks are not as thick.*

Why are termites so astounding?

Termites are social insects – they live in colonies. Some termites are also stupendous builders, making huge mound nests. The tallest known termite mound measured almost 9 m high. Amazingly, the termite workers who build such nests are blind – as are the soldiers that protect the nest from enemies. Termite queens live up to 50 years, making them the longest-lived insects.

Awesome **animals**

Life on Earth began more than 3.5 billion years ago. How life began is one of the biggest mysteries of science. More than two million kinds (species) of living things have been named – and one million of them are insects! Scientists are still finding hundreds of new species every year.

➔ *The Goliath beetle is the world's heaviest insect. It is as big as your hand and weighs up to 100 g.*

Dangerous predators

Name	Length	Weight
Killer whale	9 m	9,000 kg
Great white shark	4.5 m	3,300 kg
Estuarine crocodile	7 m	450 kg
Kodiak bear	3 m	750 kg
Siberian tiger	3.2 m	300 kg

Which animal gives birth to the biggest baby?

The blue whale, the biggest of the great whales. The blue whale is the largest living animal in the world. Its main arteries are so large that a small person could crawl through them. At birth, a blue whale calf (baby) is already 6 to 8 m long. It has to be helped to the surface to take its first breath of air – whales are mammals, not fish. Mammals are not the biggest group of animals, but they have bigger brains in relation to their body size than other animals. The lifespan of a blue whale is estimated to be 80 years. Usually they travel alone or in small groups of two to four, although off the coast of California some groups as large as 60 have been seen.

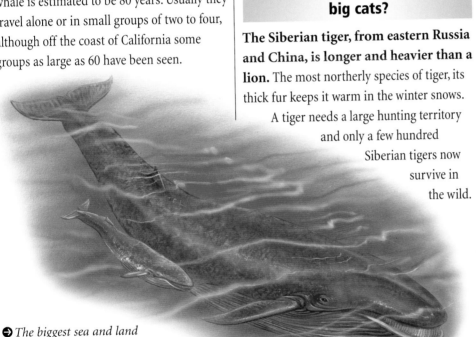

➲ *The biggest sea and land animals are mammals – the whales in the ocean and the elephants on land.*

Which is the biggest of all big cats?

The Siberian tiger, from eastern Russia and China, is longer and heavier than a lion. The most northerly species of tiger, its thick fur keeps it warm in the winter snows. A tiger needs a large hunting territory and only a few hundred Siberian tigers now survive in the wild.

● *Siberian tigers may weigh as much as 350 kg and measure 3 m in length. Tigers are only found in small regions of southern and eastern Asia. They live in a range of habitats, from tropical forests to Siberian woodlands.*

How many kinds of elephant are there?

Three. Scientists used to answer 'two': the big-eared African elephant and the smaller-eared Asiatic or Indian elephant. Recent research, however, has shown that there are in fact two species of African elephant: a bigger kind that lives on the grassy plains and a smaller kind that prefers the forest. Elephants trunks are unique among living mammals – they enable elephants to manipulate tiny objects or tear down huge tree limbs. Large, flappable ears help these huge animals to cool off in hot climates.

Speedy **sprinters**

● *Some tortoises, like this giant tortoise, may live for over 150 years.*

TOP TEN FASTEST ANIMALS

Animal	Speed
Peregrine falcon	300 km/h
Canvasback duck	110 km/h
Sailfish	109 km/h
Cheetah	100 km/h
Pronghorn antelope	100 km/h
Swift	95 km/h
Gazelle	80 km/h
Lion	80 km/h
Race horse	70 km/h
Jackrabbit	70 km/h

Why not test your knowledge on the wonders of the world! Try answering these questions to find out how much you know about the most spectacular sights on Earth, including ancient monuments, famous buildings, natural wonders, marvels of engineering and much more. Questions are grouped into the subject areas covered within the pages of this book. See how much you remember and discover how much more you can learn.

Wonders of the Ancient World

1 Which Wonder was destroyed by an earthquake?
2 Which Wonder stood at Babylon?
3 Which Wonder was found hidden under a swamp?

Puzzling Pyramids

4 What is the name of the ancient script used by the Egyptians?
5 The great sphinx has the head of a human and the body of a what?
6 How many smaller pyramids were built beside the Great Pyramid?

Marvels of Greece and Rome

8 In which mythology is Zeus the king of the Gods?
9 Which Roman arena was named after the statue Colossus?
10 Which G word was a fighting slave trained to entertain the citizens of ancient Rome?

Mysterious Monuments

11 What are the giant stone statues on Easter Island called?
12 How far did the makers of Stonehenge bring the bluestones?
13 Which ancient mound is situated near Avebury?

Forts and Castles

14 Which is the largest castle in England?
15 What is the safest part of a castle called?
16 What is the name for the water-filled ditch that is dug around castles?

17 Which German castle was the model for Walt Disney's theme park in California, USA?

Palaces and Power

18 How many rooms are there in the Forbidden City?
19 Which Palace was built for the Duke of Marlborough?
20 What was the name of the first president to live in the White House?

Walls and Towers

21 In which city is the Eiffel Tower?
22 Which Roman built a wall on the border of England and Scotland?
23 Which wall is 6,400 km long?

Built for Eternity

24 Which capital city surrounds the Vatican city?
25 In which city is the Taj Mahal?
26 In which London building is the Whispering Gallery?

7 Which rock is the temple of Abu Simbel carved from?

27 What is the name of the valley in Utah where the red sandstone rocks have been formed into dramatic shapes by the elements?

Technological Triumphs

28 What was the name of the first space shuttle?

29 What vehicles are used to move space shuttles?

30 In which year did the Thrust SSC break the sound barrier on land?

Engineering Marvels

31 In which country is the Aswan Dam?

32 What is the closest bridge to the Houses of Parliament?

33 What is the name of the longest suspension bridge?

Memorials and Mysteries

34 In which South American mountain range did the ancient Incas live?

35 Who is buried beneath the Arc de Triomphe in Paris?

36 In which US state does Mount Rushmore lie?

Awesome Landscapes

37 Which is the longest river in Africa?

38 Mount Snowdon is the highest peak in which European country?

39 Which is the world's largest desert?

Stupendous Sights

40 What is the name of the largest canyon in North America?

41 Which waterfalls were originally named 'the smoke that thunders'?

42 Which natural landmark is bigger than the US state of Texas?

Nature's Record Breakers

43 Which animal can reach speeds of over 120 km/h?

44 Which animal is 6 to 8 m long at birth?

45 What substance makes up an elephant's tusks?

Answers

1 The Colossus of Rhodes
2 The Hanging Gardens
3 The Temple of Artemis
4 Hieroglyphs
5 A lion
6 Three
7 Sandstone
8 Greek
9 The Colosseum
10 Gladiator
11 *Moai*
12 385 km

13 Silbury Hill
14 Windsor Castle
15 The Keep
16 Moat
17 Neuschwanstein Castle
18 9,000
19 Blenheim Palace
20 John Adams
21 Paris
22 Hadrian
23 The Great Wall of China
24 Rome

25 India
26 St Paul's Cathedral
27 Monument Valley
28 Columbia
29 Marion crawlers
30 1997
31 Egypt
32 Westminster Bridge
33 The Akashi Kaikyo Bridge
34 The Andes
35 The unknown soldier
36 South Dakota

37 Nile River
38 Wales
39 Sahara Desert
40 Grand Canyon
41 Victoria Falls
42 Great Barrier Reef
43 Cheetah
44 Blue whale
45 Ivory

All artworks are from Miles Kelly Artwork Bank
The Publishers would like to thank the following picture sources whose photographs appear in this book:
Page 14 (T/L) Chris Hellier/CORBIS; Page 15 (T/R) Richard A. Cooke/CORBIS;
Page 16 (T/L) Angelo Hornak/CORBIS; Page 17 (C) Hubert Stadler/CORBIS; Page 20 (T/R) Steve Raymer/CORBIS

All other photographs from:
Castrol, CMCD, Corbis, Corel, digitalSTOCK, digitalvision, Flat Earth, Hemera, ILN, John Foxx,
PhotoAlto, PhotoDisc, PhotoEssentials, PhotoPro, Stockbyte